Carpentry
making things with wood

A Puffin Book
Written and produced by McPhee Gribble Publishers
Illustrated by David Lancashire

Choosing wood

Collect second hand wood. Wooden boxes can be taken to bits or used whole as part of a construction. Some things arrive in shops packed in wooden crates or boxes. Ask shopkeepers to save them for you. Fruit and vegetable shops are likely places.

Hardware stores and timber yards cut timber for builders and often have small pieces left over. Ask if you can look in the scrap heap. Visit building sites and ask the foreman for spare pieces of wood.

Take this book with you on your timber hunts so that people can see what you are after.

Work out how much wood you need for your carpentry job and make a list. Don't choose planks that are too thick. They will be hard to saw through and heavy to carry.

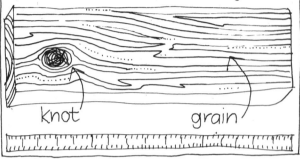

pick wood without too many knots

knot   grain

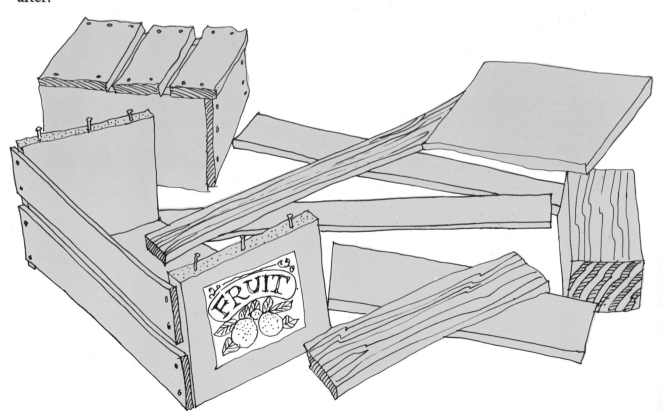

FRUIT

The two main kinds of timber are hardwood and softwood. Hardwood is not only hard to cut and nail but heavy. Ask for softwood whenever possible.

Plywood, chipboard and hardboard are made in factories from small chips of wood or very thin layers glued together. They can be bought in sheets. Some kinds are not easy to saw or nail – so check before you choose them for a job.

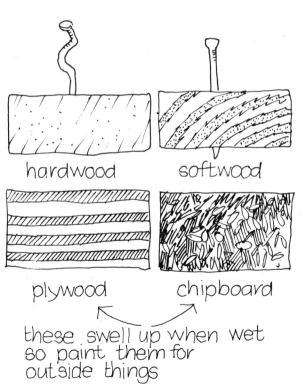

hardwood is very much stronger than softwood

hardwood

softwood

plywood

chipboard

these swell up when wet so paint them for outside things

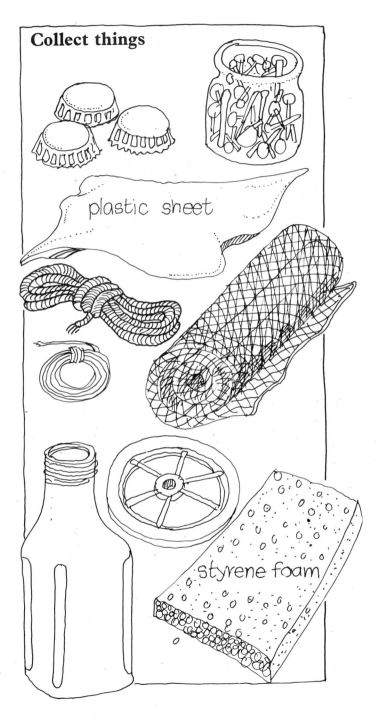

Collect things

plastic sheet

styrene foam

Tools

There are lots of things you can make with just a hammer, a saw and nails. If you have to buy tools start with these. Get the strongest you can.

Hammer

Before hammering check your position so you can hold the wood firmly. Work on a flat surface.

Hold the hammer near the end of the handle. Keep the hammer head facing straight down onto the top of the nail – if you hit the nail even a bit to one side it will bend. Once a nail has bent badly it is better to pull it out and start again.

Nails

Choose the right nails for the job you are doing. Measure the length against the pieces of wood you are nailing together.

For most jobs the nail should go through the top piece and halfway into the bottom piece of wood.

Sometimes for extra strength you can use nails that go right through both pieces. Then you bash the point over with the hammer. But make sure you are nailing over a soft surface – earth or a spare piece of wood.

For nailing thin planks use thin nails or the wood will split.

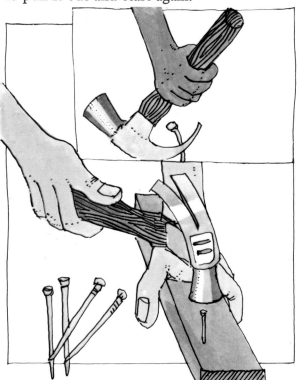

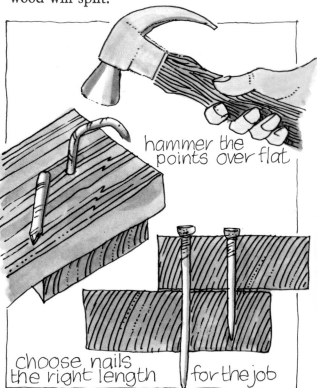

hammer the points over flat

choose nails the right length for the job

Saw

tenon saw –
this is the easiest to use

panel saw

Sawing is always hard work but it is easier if you hold the wood you are cutting quite still.

A carpenter's work bench has a clamp or vice to do this.

If you haven't a clamp you can use your foot or knee to hold the wood still – or get someone to stand on one end with both feet. Use a low table or a step to rest the wood on. Stick the part to be sawn off just over the edge.

kneel on the wood to hold it quite still

line up a corner to draw straight across

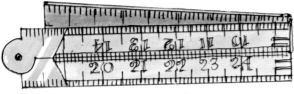

Use a ruler and pencil to mark the lengths you want. A folding carpenter's rule makes measuring long boards easy.

Ladder

T s ladder will not be strong enough for cli bing very high on, but it would be use l for leaning on low tree branches or for eaching bunks or cupboards.

You will need 2 long pieces of wood for the sides of the ladder and short pieces for the steps.

The sides should be about as tall as you.

All different shapes and sizes will do for the steps. Put the thinnest near the bottom so if they break you won't have far to fall.

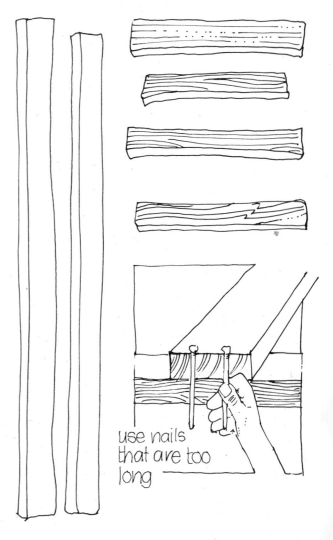

use nails that are too long

Let the steps stick over the edge so the nails aren't too near the ends.

Use 2 nails in each joint but not in line along the grain of the wood.

place them like this to make the joints stiff

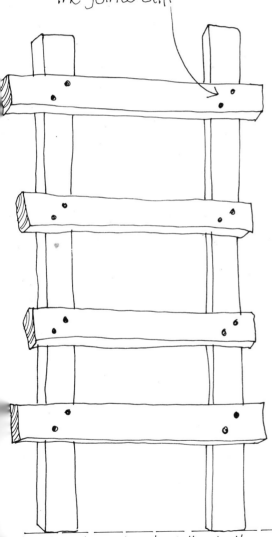

ake the sides level at the bottom or the ladder will wobble

bang the points flat

If you want a taller ladder make it much stronger by using screws instead of nails.

Bird tray

This is a tray for holding birdseed or breadcrumbs. Put it outside but near a window so you can watch the birds feeding.

Find a piece of timber for the base or nail small boards across 2 bars of wood. Bits of fruit box would do.

It can go in a tree, on a balcony or on a post in the garden.

Even if there aren't many birds around at first more will come every day as they find the food.

The tray should be large enough for a lot of small birds to fit on.

The tray needs a rim to stop the food scattering.

You will need 4 small boards about 2 cm thick. Measure them against the base to find the right length. Allow a ledge all round for the birds to land on.

cut the sides to the length you have marked

Nail the rim to the base.

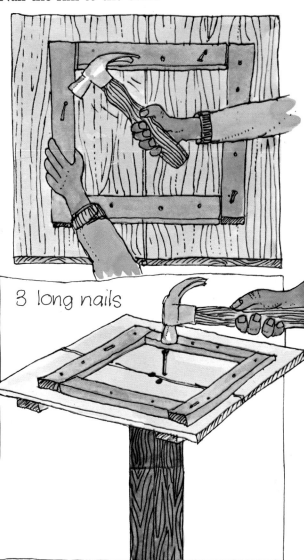

3 long nails

put the tray where the birds can see creeping cats

A cage for a small animal

Make a simple cage out of wooden boxes then add some special details to suit your small animal.

Wooden boxes, like the ones fruit or wine bottles are packed in, make quick cages. You may need more than one to get enough wood.

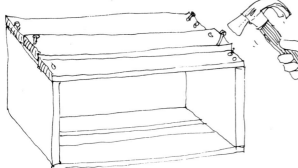

Strengthen the edges of the box with extra bars of wood if they are too thin to nail into.

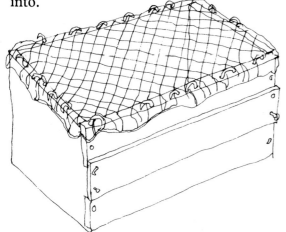

Wire netting is fastened on with thin nails bent over, or with staples.

Gaps between the boards can be covered with extra boards nailed on, or with wire netting. Make sure that the top of the cage won't let in rain.

Once you have made your cage animal-proof, add some ideas of your own.

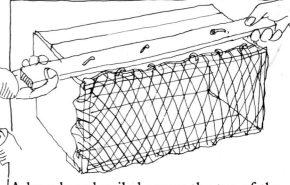

A long board nailed across the top of the cage makes it easy to carry.

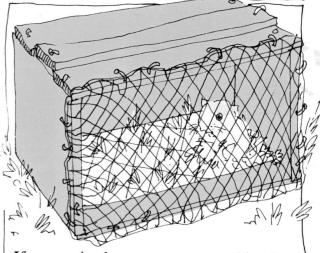

If your animal eats grass, you could pull off one of the boards on the bottom of the cage. Cover the gap in wire netting nailed on firmly.

Make a door in the cage by nailing short boards across 2 bars of wood.

Cut a hole in the back of the cage the same size as your door or a bit smaller.

Strong plastic or cloth can be used for hinges or cut up an old leather belt.

Make the door open downwards so the animal can't rush out. Bend over nails for door catches.

Make an extra room from another box the same height.

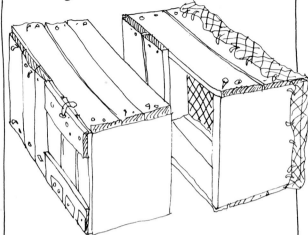

With the openings together join the boxes with strips of wood nailed on.

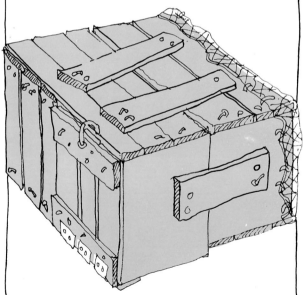

Put something inside the extra room for the animal to sleep on.

Musical instrument

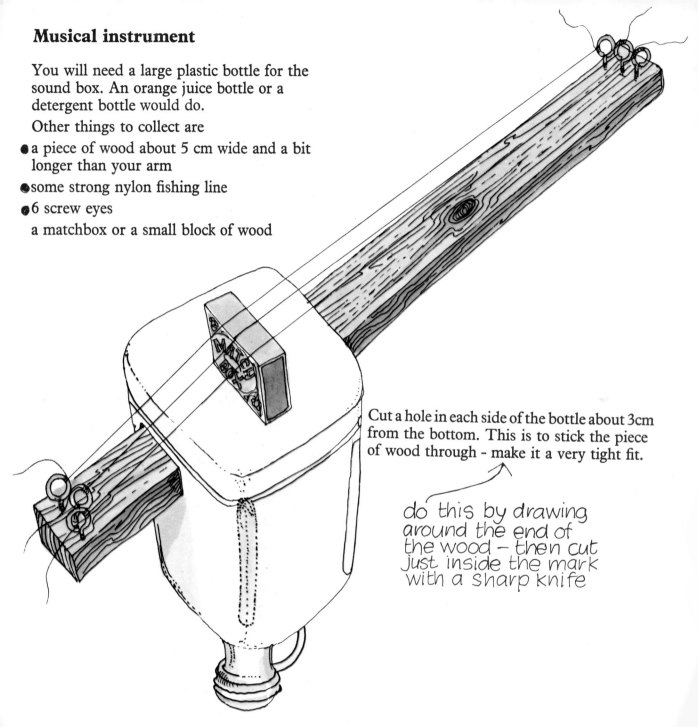

You will need a large plastic bottle for the sound box. An orange juice bottle or a detergent bottle would do.

Other things to collect are

- a piece of wood about 5 cm wide and a bit longer than your arm
- some strong nylon fishing line
- 6 screw eyes

  a matchbox or a small block of wood

Cut a hole in each side of the bottle about 3cm from the bottom. This is to stick the piece of wood through - make it a very tight fit.

do this by drawing around the end of the wood — then cut just inside the mark with a sharp knife

With a hammer and a small nail make a shallow hole for each screw eye. Evenly space 3 at each end of the wood.

Tie 3 strands of fishing line tightly between the pairs of screw eyes. Allow plenty of extra length in the strands so you can knot them easily.

Slip the matchbox or block of wood under the strings on the end of the bottle.

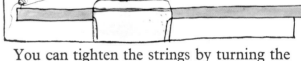

You can tighten the strings by turning the screw eyes.

When the strings are plucked the sound waves bounce around inside the empty bottle and make the sounds louder.

Push the wood through with the nail holes turned towards the bottom of the bottle.

Screw the eyes into their holes.

Platform

This platform is strong enough to walk around on. You can use it for lots of things.

Haul it up a tree and use it as a tree house floor.

Tie on empty kerosene tins or blocks of styrene foam to make a raft.

Prop it up on 4 supports and make a stage in the garden.

You can use second hand timber or buy pieces cut to the right size – ask for softwood called radiata pine. This is easy to nail and light to carry.

For a basic platform 1 metre square you will need

- 5 pieces of timber about 75 mm wide, 25 mm thick and 1 metre long
- 9 or 10 thin planks, 1 metre long, to cover the platform
- Lots of 50 mm nails

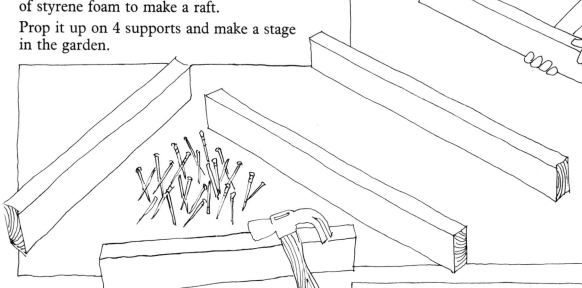

Lay 3 beams out on the ground. The 2 outside beams should be exactly a metre apart, outside edge to outside edge. Put the centre beam where you guess the middle is.

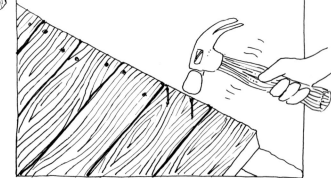

Starting at one end nail the planks across the beams – 2 nails through each plank into each beam.

but change the lengths to suit the platform size you need

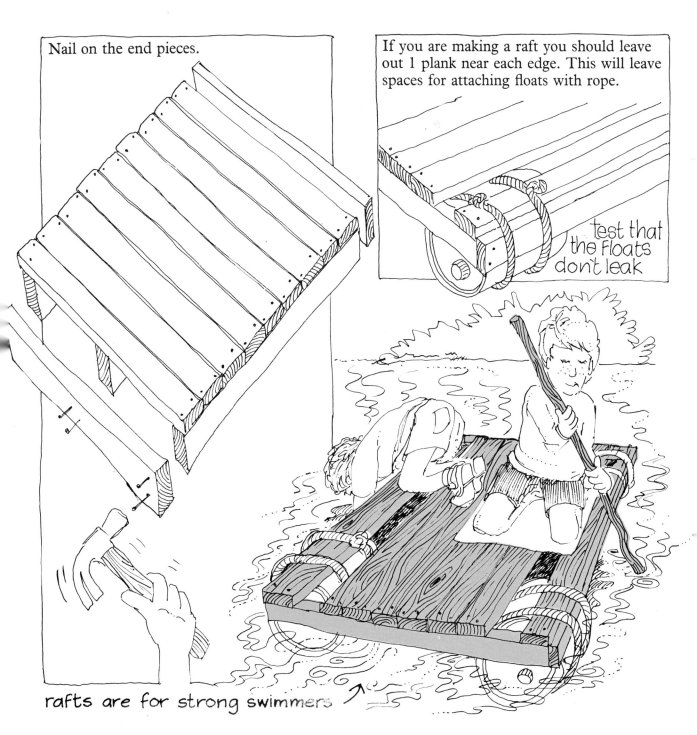

Nail on the end pieces.

If you are making a raft you should leave out 1 plank near each edge. This will leave spaces for attaching floats with rope.

test that the floats don't leak

rafts are for strong swimmers ↑

Gumboot remover

You will need a thick plank about 25 cm wide and 60 cm long.

Cut a heel sized notch with a saw in the edge of the wood.

Dig a hole and bury over half the plank in the ground by an outside door. It should stick up at an angle. Pack the earth back firmly.

Tambourine stick

Nail bottle tops in twos and threes loosely to the bottom end of a square stick or broom handle.

Foot scraper

You will need 2 wooden scrubbing brushes, old bottle tops, scraps of wood.

Cut 2 rectangular pieces of wood a bit bigger than the backs of the scrubbing brushes.

Nail them to the brushes.

On a larger piece of wood mark where the brushes will go to fit around a foot.

Nail bottle tops edge up between the marks.

Drill holes in the large piece and the brush boards and screw them together.

Storage jars

These are very useful above a work bench or desk. Collect some screw top jars. Nail the lids to the underside of a shelf or cupboard. Screw the jars into their lids.

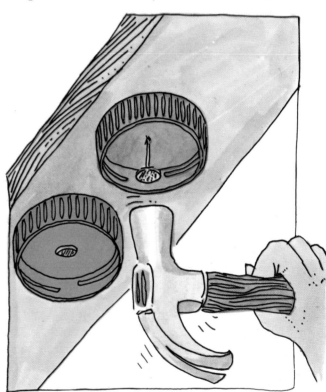

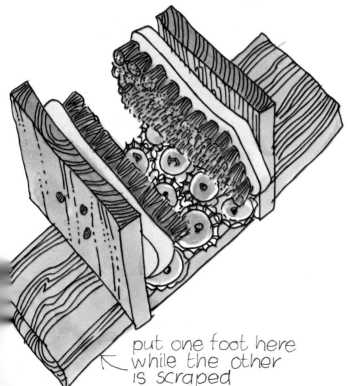

put one foot here while the other is scraped

nail a set to a plank for giving away

More tools

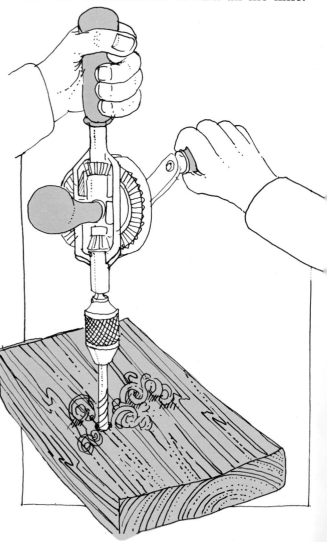

hand drill

brace

← bits →

Hold the handle of the drill in your left hand and press down gently. Keep the drill straight.

Drilling and screwing makes a stronger joint than nailing and is less likely to split the wood.

If you have a drill and enjoy using it you can use screws instead of nails all the time.

The size of the bit is chosen to fit the screws you are using.

Before you start to drill make a small dent with a nail to mark the position of the hole. This will make a nest for the point of the drill.

The chuck is turned to release the jaws of the drill then tightened to hold the drill bit firmly.

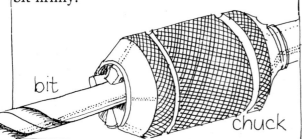

bit

chuck

Screws

Choose the kind of screw that suits the job you are doing. A flat-headed wood screw will usually be best. The screw should go well into the wood but not stick out the other side.

Screwdriver

Use one that fits the top of the screw.

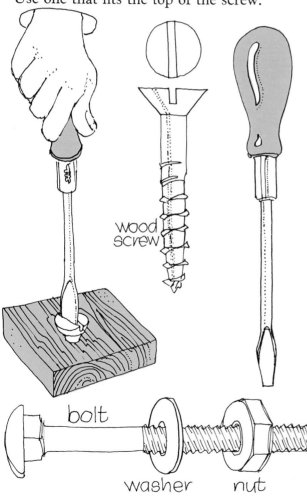

wood screw

bolt

washer   nut

Finishing off

For smoothing off splintery surfaces use a medium grade sandpaper. Make a sandpaper block with an offcut.

You can use almost any kind of paint for decorating the things you make.

Read the label on paint you use to see if you will need turpentine for cleaning brushes. If it is plastic paint you will only need water. Give the paint a good stir with a stick before you start.

paint things

old cloth for drips

Stilts

You will need 2 long thin pieces of wood about as tall as you.

They must be strong enough to take your weight without bending and thin enough for you to close your hand around. Old broom handles would do.

For foot rests you will need 2 blocks of wood wide enough to take your foot.

Offcuts from a timber yard work well.

Get more than you need as short fat bits of wood split easily.

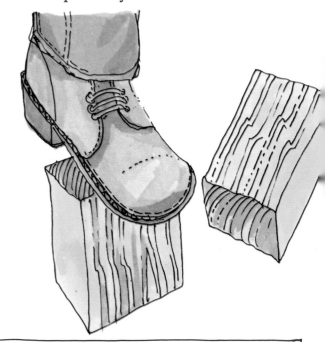

Coach bolts and wing nuts are the best way to fasten stilts together. Choose 4 coach bolts long enough to go right through the stilt handles and the foot blocks.

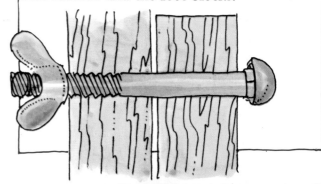

Use a bit the right size for your bolts and drill 2 holes through each foot block.

Hold each foot block in its position. Use a pencil or a long nail to make a mark through each hole on to the handle. Drill 2 holes in each handle.

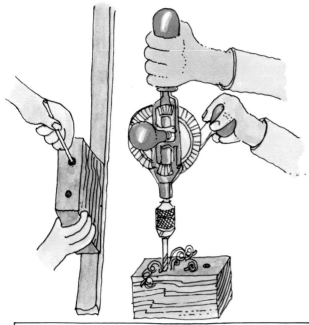

Bolt the blocks on to the handles and screw the wing nuts on tightly.

this takes practice

Wind vane

A wind vane tells you the direction the wind is blowing in. It has a sail that swings a pointer into the wind.

You will need
- a piece of wooden rod (dowel) about as long as your arm and 2 or 3 cm thick
- 2 flat boards for the base
- a fat cotton reel of wood or plastic
- 1 very long nail (10 cm)
- some stiff plastic for the sail and pointer
- a clamp or a strong friend to hold the rod still while you saw and drill

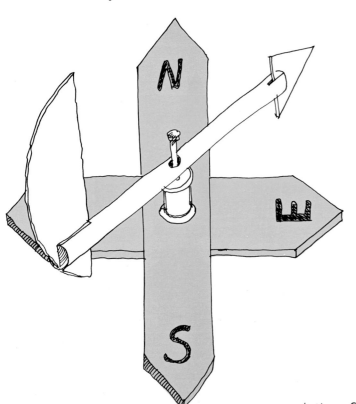

Saw the 2 flat boards into points at both ends.

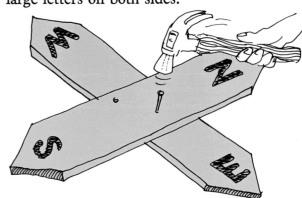

Nail them together to make the base. Mark north, south, east and west in large letters on both sides.

Cut out the sail and the pointer with a sharp knife.

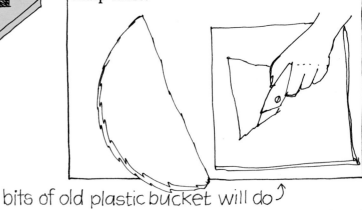

bits of old plastic bucket will do ↗

Cut notches in the wooden rod – a long one for the sail and a shorter one for the pointer. Test them to make sure they fit. If they are too loose fix them with glue.

a clamp is even better than a foot

Find the spot where the rod balances. Hang it from a piece of string and move the string until the rod hangs level. Mark this position with a pencil.

Drill a hole through the rod where you have marked. Use a bit in your drill that is a little fatter than the long nail. This lets the pointer swing free in the wind.

Drill through the centre of the base but use a drill bit smaller than before for a tight fit.

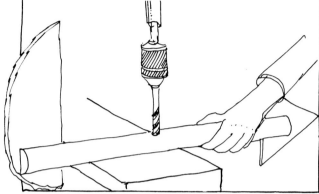

Thread the long nail through the rod and the cotton reel then hammer it through the base.

Now find a windy place as high as you can get – a fence post or a wooden balcony rail works well. Make sure your north mark on the base faces north. Or find west as the sun goes down.

Now hammer the nail again to hold the wind vane in position.

Billy cart

A billy cart can be made from second hand timber.

You will also need
4 wheels
2 steel axle rods to fit them, about 50 cm long
1 long strong bolt with 2 nuts and 4 washers

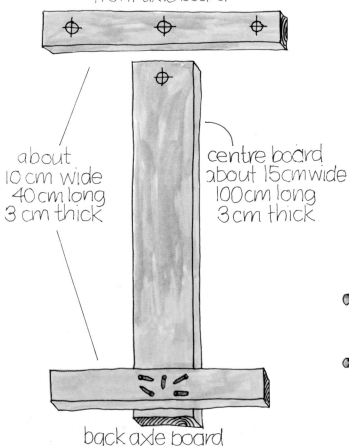

front axle board

about
10 cm wide
40 cm long
3 cm thick

centre board
about 15 cm wide
100 cm long
3 cm thick

back axle board

Nail the back axle board under the end of the centre board. Use nails that are too long and bash the ends over.

the drill bit should be slightly fatter than the bolt you have

Drill 3 holes in the front axle board – one in the middle and one near each end.

Drill a hole in the middle of the centre board about 10 cm from the front end.

Attach the axle rods to their boards. Use long nails and bend them over the rod. On the front axle board put the rod to one side of the drilled holes.

You can get special wheels called ball races from truck wreckers. They are fast and noisy on concrete paths. If you use these you won't need axle rods, just fat axle boards sharpened at the ends and jammed in.

Bolt the front axle board to the centre board. Test that it will swivel freely.

See what you can find or make for a seat – like a plastic tub with one side cut out.

Sit on the frame so your feet reach the front axle comfortably. Mark the position and nail or screw the seat on.

bolt

washer

2 washers

washer

2 nuts

Find some strong cord for a steering rope. Thread it through the holes in the front board and knot the ends.

Fit the wheels on the axles. Thread a nail through the hole in the end of the rod – bend it around to hold the wheel on.

bang with the hammer

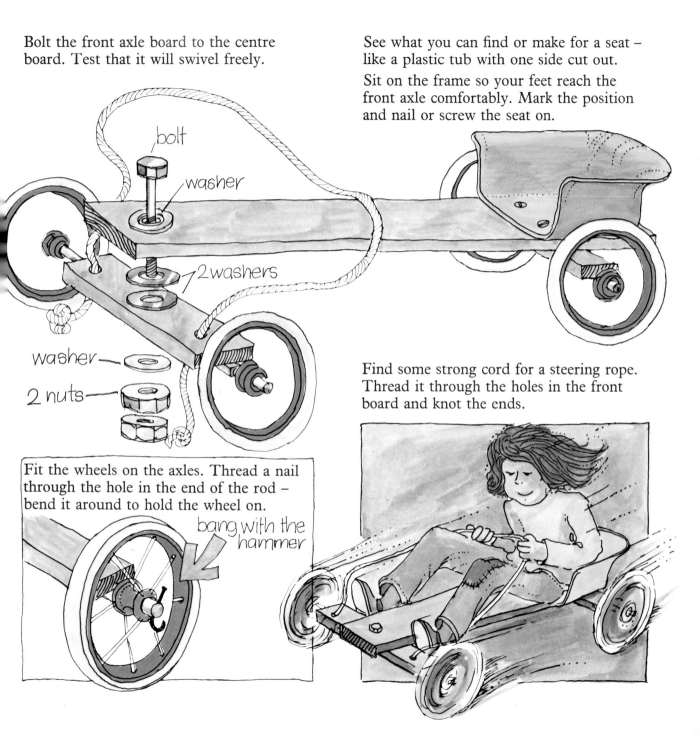

A-frame

An A-frame shape can be used to make many things. A hut, a rabbit hutch, a chicken coop, a bicycle shelter are just a few uses it could have.

The frame is made with triangles. You can use a collection of old thin wood because a triangle is such a strong shape.

The length of the sides of the triangle will depend on what you are using the frame for. Measure the height and width you need before you start.

To make 2 triangles you will need

- 2 pieces of wood for the bases cut to the same length
- 4 pieces of wood for the sides cut to the same length
- 2 scraps of wood for joining the sides at the top

Nail a side on to each end of the base. Use 1 nail in each end.

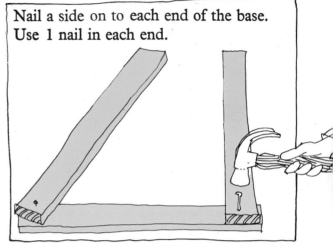

Turn the frame over and lean the sides in until their corners just touch.

Nail the scrap of wood across them with 2 nails in each side.

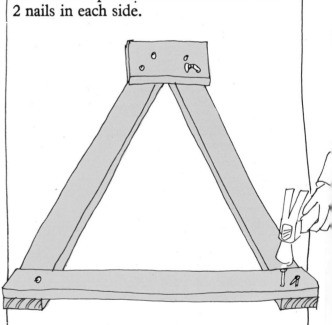

Now put another nail into each bottom joint to make them firm.

When you have made 2 triangles the same size you can join them together.

Nail a board across from top to top. Prop the triangles up while you do this with something heavy on each side – a garbage bin and a wheelbarrow would do, or a friend.

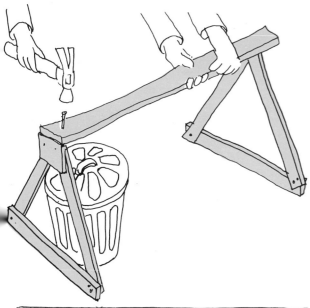

Now fill in the sides of the frame to suit what you want it for. You will need some boards and some wire netting for a hutch, maybe some hardboard or plastic sheeting for a hut or bicycle shelter.

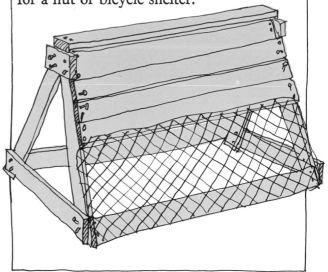

Lightly nail a brace across each side to stiffen the frame while you finish it. You can take this off later if you like.

Nail boards to join the triangles at the bottom.

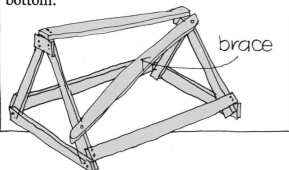

brace

An easel needs long nails on each side to support a piece of hardboard. You could make a double easel for painting with a friend.

Chair

This is a plan for a sturdy chair. You will need to take a lot of care measuring and sawing straight.

The chair can be made with a hammer and nails but it will be very wobbly until all the the pieces are nailed on.

Use a drill and screws instead of nails if you like. This would make the chair stronger too.

Once you have made a chair, you could work out how to make a table to match using the same method.

You could buy the timber for your chair or collect scraps. This is what you will need altogether.

- 350 cm of narrow softwood (50 mm × 25 mm)
- 140 cm of wider softwood (75 mm × 25 mm)

(use these measurements as a guide - the wood can be fatter or thinner)

- wide boards or a square of plywood for the seat
- lots of 50 mm nails

1 Saw off 6 pieces of the narrow timber, each exactly 35 cm long. Then saw 2 longer pieces, both exactly 70 cm.

Saw off 4 pieces of the wider timber, each exactly 35 cm long.

2 Join 2 of the short narrow pieces with 1 of the wider pieces. These are the front legs.

Before you nail test that the legs are straight with the square corner of a book. Use 2 nails in each end.

3 Join the 2 long narrow pieces with 1 of the wider pieces. This makes the back legs and the back rest. Measure the length of the legs against the front ones you have made. Use 2 nails in each end.

this will be
← the backrest

make all the legs the same leng

4 Join the front and back legs together at the sides using the last 2 wider pieces.

Fit the side pieces between the ends you left sticking out and nail through the ends as well as the sides.

nail through the ends as well as the sides

6 Nail the last 2 narrow pieces across the top of the back rest.

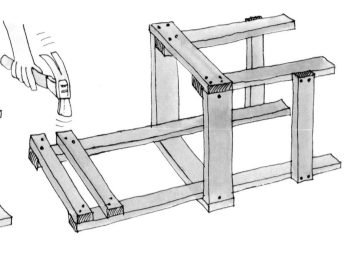

When you are hammering make sure the frame is firmly supported or it will fall to bits.

5 Nail a short narrow piece between the legs on both sides. Put them close to the bottom to support the legs.

7 Nail wide boards or a square of plywood onto the frame to make the seat.

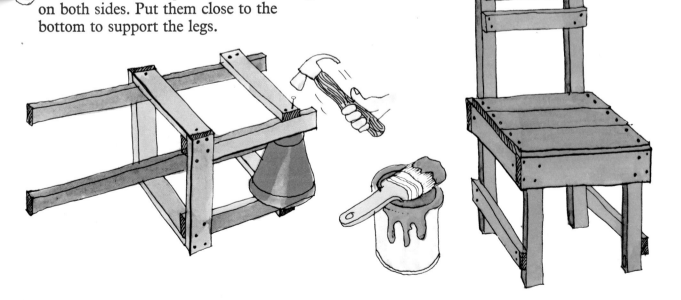

Coping saw

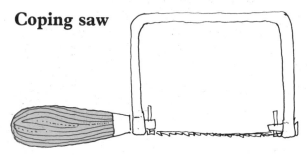

This is used for cutting curves in timber. The thin blade and the open frame let you cut in any direction you like. Quite thick softwood can be sawn into shapes.

A clamp or a vice to hold the wood perfectly still makes sawing easy. If your wood is very thin, like plywood, you could manage with a friend holding it firm.

Try not to twist the blade as you saw – it will break. Have some spare blades ready.

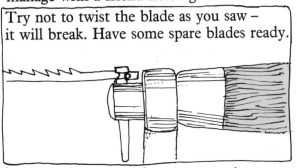

the teeth must face away from the handle

Keep changing the position of the wood in the clamp so you are cutting the curve in the way you find easiest.

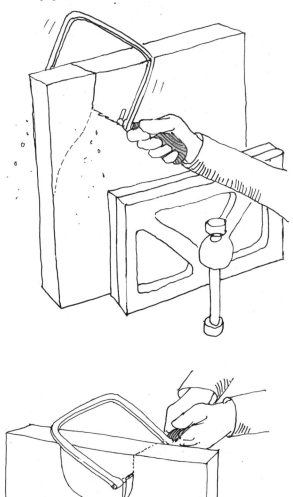

You will be able to think of lots of shapes you could cut out with a coping saw. These are a few.

Dartboard or target

On a piece of soft fibre board draw a large circle. A rubbish bin lid might be the right size to draw around.

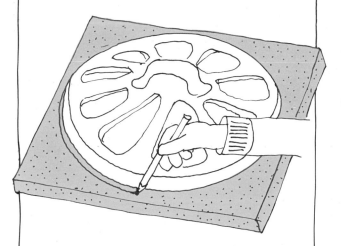

Cut it out with a coping saw and paint it in a dartboard or target pattern.

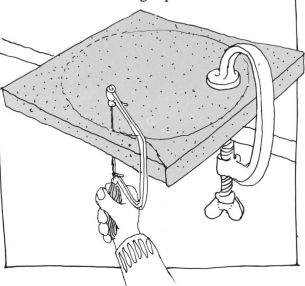

Jigsaw puzzle

Find a picture printed on strong paper – or draw one.

Glue it to a piece of plywood the same size.

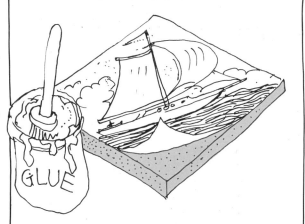

When the glue is quite dry use a coping saw to cut the picture into small curvy pieces.

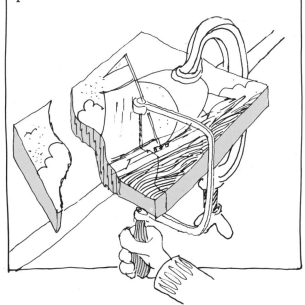

Sandals

To make sandals you will need

- a piece of smooth softwood big enough for 2 feet and fairly thick
- 2 strips of cloth – bits of old jeans look good
- some tacks with big heads

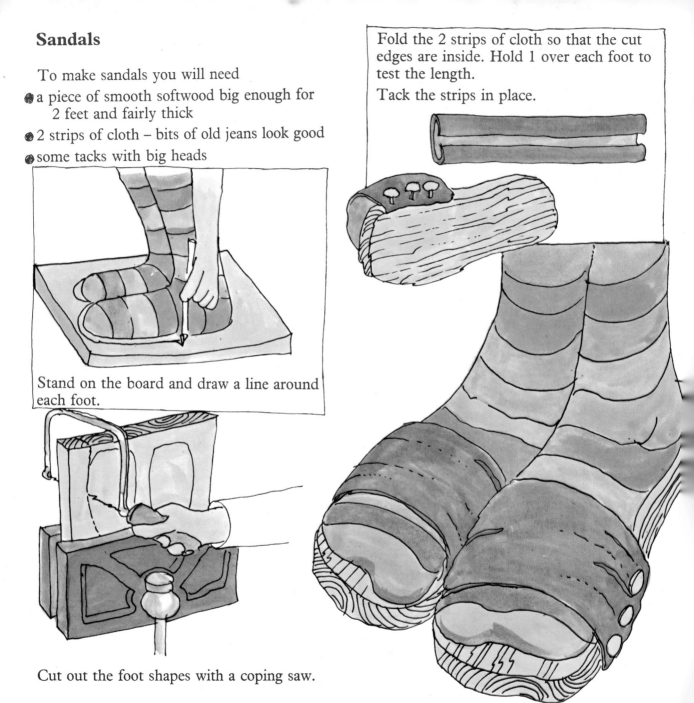

Stand on the board and draw a line around each foot.

Cut out the foot shapes with a coping saw.

Fold the 2 strips of cloth so that the cut edges are inside. Hold 1 over each foot to test the length.

Tack the strips in place.